NATURAL RESOURCES

Sally Morgan

Contents

Introduction

Every day, more than 200,000 babies are born in the world. During their lifetime they will use up resources. As babies they will need water, food and clothes. As they grow older, they will use even more resources – building materials for a home, fuel for a car, electricity to power an array of electrical goods, and much more. The fuel and the raw materials to make all these goods come from natural resources. A natural resource is a useful material that occurs naturally. Examples include wood, water, metals, coal and oil.

People have used the world's natural resources for thousands of years – for example, water has been used for drinking and watering crops and wood has been used for fuel. More recently fossil fuels (coal, oil and gas) have been used for generating electricity, and iron is used to make steel. Precious gems

▲ Power stations need a fuel in order to generate electricity. The most commonly used fuel is coal, although other resources such as oil, gas and wood can also be used.

such as diamonds are resources too, as are metals such as aluminium and gold.

Global resources

Natural resources occur around the world, but they are not distributed equally. Some countries have more resources than others. Oil deposits are found in the Middle East and in parts of North America, while rich seams (layers) of coal are found in Europe and China. South Africa has large deposits of coal, gold and diamonds, but Malawi, a nearby country, has very few natural resources.

A country's natural resources can play an important role in its economic development, wealth and status in the world. Today, European countries, together with the United States, Canada and Russia, are among the richest in the world and can influence development elsewhere. Major oil-producing countries such as Saudi Arabia are also influential. Nations such as China and India are developing quickly and their growing demands are putting pressure on resources and pushing up the costs.

Trade in resources

Over the last 50 years or so, communications and transport links have opened up international trade. The volume of this trade has increased greatly too. Globalisation is making available new resources in some of the more remote parts of the world – hardwoods now come from forests in Papua New Guinea, oil and other valuable minerals from central African countries such as Gabon and the Democratic Republic of the Congo.

This increase in trade is harming the world's environment as it results in more pollution.

▲ Iron ore is much in demand by the iron and steel industry. The ore is bulky so it has to be transported around the world by sea.

In addition, much of this trade is unsustainable. The reserves (the amounts available) of resources such as oil or copper will not last forever. In some areas, resources such as wood are being used up much more quickly than they can be replaced.

In this book you will find out about the different types of resources that are traded, where they come from and how they are obtained. You will also learn about the benefits and drawbacks of globalisation in this area, and how the problems can be tackled.

Wealth from the Ground

Many of the natural resources used in industry come from below the ground. Rocks such as limestone and bauxite can be quarried from just beneath the surface, while coal can be reached by mines. Oil is obtained by drilling a well and pumping it out.

Oil exploration

Oil is formed over hundreds of millions of years from the remains of microscopic organisms that dropped to the bottom of the sea. The remains became buried under layers of sediment such as silt and mud. As the layers built up, the temperatures and pressures increased, the sediment turned to rock and the remains were changed into oil and gas.

▼ Nodding donkeys are used in onshore oil fields to bring oil to the surface. The up/down movement of the nodding donkey powers a pump at the bottom of the well. Each stroke can bring as much as 40 litres of crude oil to the surface.

When oil is discovered, further exploration has to take place to work out the extent of the oil field and the amount of oil in the ground. Usually the potential oil-producing areas are divided up into blocks and each block is leased to an oil company. The oil companies carry out detailed surveys to locate the oil, often using seismology. When searching for oil on land, special vehicles with heavy metal plates thump the ground to create vibrations that pass through the earth. The returning echoes are recorded.

Focus on...
Oil reserves

The Middle East is the world's greatest oil-producing region, especially Saudi Arabia and the countries lying beside the Persian Gulf. The other major producers are Russia, the United States and Mexico. Over the last 20 years or so, the estimated reserves of oil have increased substantially as a result of more exploration. In 2006, the estimated oil reserves were 1,300 billion barrels, of which about 70 per cent was in the Middle East and Canada. Oil production has increased each year – today it is double what it was in 1960. However, experts estimate that the production rate will peak sometime in the next 10 years and then start to fall.

▲ Offshore oil can be located by conducting underwater seismic surveys. Oil companies use unmanned AUVs (Autonomous Underwater Vehicles) and the data from the survey is transmitted back to the control centre for analysis.

By studying the recordings, experts can work out the location of the oil.

To reach the oil, a well has to be drilled down through the layers of rock. Test holes are drilled in the most likely places. If sufficient oil is found, the company may decide to develop the oil field. Crude oil is pumped to the surface and then moved by either tanker or pipeline to refineries. At the refinery, the oil is heated to separate the different substances mixed with it, such as gasoline, diesel, aviation fuel, bitumen and kerosene.

Natural gas

Another important fossil fuel is natural gas. This is a mix of gases including methane and propane. Natural gas is found in the ground, in the same way as oil. Often it is found near oil fields and coal seams. Natural gas is pumped to the surface and piped to storage tanks. It is then processed to separate the different gases. The main problem with natural gas is transportation. It can be piped great distances across land – for example, there are long pipelines carrying gas from Russia to Europe and from Alaska to the rest of North America. However, to be transported across oceans it has to be compressed to form liquefied natural gas, which can be moved by tanker.

Have your say

The Arctic National Wildlife Refuge in Alaska is one of the few unspoilt wilderness areas in the United States. Oil lies under the ground here, though. Conservationists claim that oil exploration will scare away animals and say there may be oil spills. The oil companies argue that only five per cent of the land will be used for oil wells.

- Should oil companies be allowed to drill for oil in the Arctic National Wildlife Refuge?
- New technology makes it possible to drill an angled oil well. Would it be acceptable to drill an angled oil well from outside the refuge?
- The oil would bring new jobs to the area. Which is more important – jobs or wildlife?

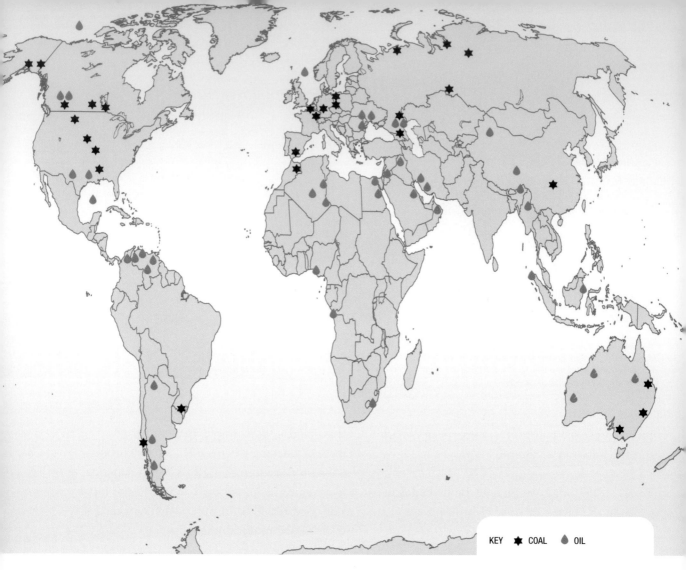

KEY ★ COAL ● OIL

▲ This map shows the main areas of the world where coal and oil can be found.

Quarrying

Rocks such as limestone and granite lie close to the surface of the ground and can be reached by quarrying. First the overlying soil is removed to reveal the layers of rock. The rock is carefully blown up using dynamite, then the blocks of rock are moved by large machinery and placed on huge dumper trucks. The blocks may be crushed into smaller pieces and taken for further processing.

Some valuable metals do not occur in a pure form in the ground and so they have to be separated from the ore in which they are found. For example, aluminium must be refined from an ore called bauxite. The bauxite is quarried and crushed, and then transported to a refinery. There the rock is heated and the aluminium extracted. Another important ore is iron ore. Iron ore is taken from quarries to blast furnaces, where it is heated with coke and limestone to make iron. Iron can be made into steel by adding a small amount of carbon.

Coal mining

Coal occurs in seams in the ground. If the coal lies close to the surface it can be reached by strip mining, where the coal is literally dug out of the ground. The overlying layers of rock and soil, called overburden, are removed and piled to one side. Then the coal is removed. The mine advances along the coal seam and the overburden is used to fill the hole behind. Where the coal seams are deep in the ground, shafts have to be dug down to the seam and then tunnels dug along the seam. These are called deep mines. In Europe and North America, deep mines employ a skilled workforce that uses hi-tech equipment to remove the coal. The productivity of such mines has almost doubled over the last 30 years, while the number of miners has more than halved. In contrast, in countries such as India and China there is a huge workforce mining coal.

Coal is a bulky material and it is moved mostly by sea or by train. Its main use is as a fuel for power stations. Often the power stations are built close to coal mines so the coal does not have to be moved very far.

Focus on...
Aluminium

Aluminium can be used to create strong but lightweight metal products such as drinks cans, ladders, garden furniture and machinery. However, refining aluminium is very damaging to the environment. Bauxite tends to be found in tropical areas, often under rainforests, which the quarries destroy. The refining process is energy-hungry. It is far more environmentally friendly to recycle aluminium. Scrap aluminium is heated until it melts; it is then rolled into sheets and used to make new products. Recycling aluminium uses just five per cent of the energy needed to refine aluminium from bauxite.

Eyewitness

'It's about time the government intervened to save our remaining coal industry. The coal reserves in this country are a valuable resource that will long outlive North Sea gas. Modern coal technology is well able to make this a clean energy source; it is the fuel of the future, not just the past.'
Keith Wilson, United Kingdom

'Coal mining should stop. The fuel is dirty. The job of mining is dangerous and almost inhuman. Natural gas is an easy replacement fuel. Clean and easy to convert.'
Anton Jansen, Australia

▲ Much of the world's gold is found in hard rock. The gold-rich rock is mined using similar techniques to those used in coal mining. Australia, South Africa and the United States are the largest producers of gold.

A History of Using Natural Resources

One feature that separates humans from other animals is their ability to use tools and to alter their environment to make it more suitable for their needs. This has involved the use of natural resources.

Many thousands of years ago, early man used wood to create shelters and to make fires for warmth and cooking food. People made clothes out of animal skins and collected flints from the ground to use as simple tools. Since this time an ever-increasing range of natural resources has been used by humans.

The importance of bronze

It was the use of simple tools and wood that led to the first use of metals about 7,000 years ago – the start of a period known as the Bronze Age. Bronze is made from heating copper and tin together. It is strong and hard, and it was much in demand for making objects, especially weapons. About 5,000 years ago the raw materials needed to make bronze were traded around the Mediterranean, together with charcoal, which was used to heat the copper. So much copper and tin had been used that by 3,700 years ago there were shortages of these metals and copper items were recycled. People started looking for alternatives. Copper had been used rather than iron because it had a lower melting point and could be extracted more easily.

However, the shortages forced people in present-day Turkey to develop a technique of extracting iron from iron ore. The iron was used to make weapons, utensils and as supports in shelters.

The Industrial Revolution

For centuries, wood was used as a fuel for cooking and heating water, and for constructing buildings and ships. Large areas of forest were cleared to provide the wood. However, during the eighteenth century two other resources became important to economic development – coal and iron.

This was a time of invention, when industrial machines began to be used and industry became far more efficient. This period was called the Industrial Revolution. It started in Britain and spread to the rest of Europe, the United States and beyond. Historians believe that the Industrial Revolution began in Britain because the country had plenty of natural resources, in particular coal, and because of its trade with its colonies around the world. During this time the use of coal and iron increased greatly, and many mines were built in Europe and in the United States. One of the most important inventions was the steam engine, in which coal was burnt and the heat used to make steam. The steam was used to power machinery.

▲ This illustration shows coal being hauled to the surface from a shallow mine during the Industrial Revolution. Coal was an important fuel during this time, as it was used to drive much of the new machinery being used in industry.

Focus on...
Copper

During the 1800s the United Kingdom led the world in smelting copper. The British had established many trade routes around the world and about three-quarters of the world's copper ore was shipped to the United Kingdom for smelting. It was then traded with the rest of the world to be used for protective copper plating on the wooden hulls of ships, for making bells, saucepans, coins and for decoration. British control of the copper market declined as it became more economic to build smelters near the mines. Large deposits of copper ore were found in Australia, Chile and the United States. Today there is a valuable global trade in copper, and its two main uses are in the circuit boards of electronic equipment and for plumbing (pipes and water cylinders). The demand for copper is increasing and estimates suggest that all known copper reserves will be depleted by 2050.

▲ Sheets of copper are stacked ready for transportation at Chiquicamata in Chile, one of the world's largest copper mines.

Black gold

One of the most important resources to influence the world was oil. Crude oil had long been collected from places where it seeped out of the ground, but the drilling of wells did not occur until the mid-1800s. The first commercial oil well in the United States was dug by Edwin Drake in 1859, in Pennsylvania. He used a hand pump to bring the oil to the surface. At first the oil was used to produce kerosene, which was used in lamps instead of whale oil. Later it was used by industry and in engines. This was the start of the oil boom in the United States. Between 1899 and 1906 production doubled, from just over 57 million barrels to 126 million barrels. It has been increasing steadily ever since.

Changing trade

Technological developments over the last 50 years have led to trade in different resources, such as uranium for nuclear power stations, titanium for paint and as an alloy in aircraft, spacecraft, military vehicles and missiles, and tantalum for electronic components.

At the same time, trade in well-established resources such as coal is changing. In Europe, there have been widespread closures of deep coal mines, especially in the United Kingdom and Romania. There are several reasons for

▼ Since 1998 the coal industry in Romania has been completely reorganised and unprofitable mines have been closed. The number of miners has fallen from 175,000 to just over 40,000.

this. The operating costs are high, so only the most accessible seams can be mined profitably. Also coal produces polluting gases when it is burnt, especially lignite, a poor-quality coal found in many central European countries. Another reason is the switch to natural gas in power stations, because natural gas burns more cleanly than coal. Often coal is imported from countries where production costs are cheaper. Traditionally coal mines have employed a lot of people. When a mine is closed, the effects on the surrounding community can be long-term. The majority of the workforce becomes unemployed and many experience difficulty in finding alternative employment. Other businesses suffer, as there is no money being spent in the local community. Undoubtedly more changes lie ahead as the global market develops, so communities have to be flexible and able to adapt. Governments can help by investing in training and giving grants to enable new businesses to develop.

Have your say

Coal mines in many European countries are being closed and coal is being imported from other parts of the world.

- Is it better to keep the mines open and expect people to pay more for the coal, or should cheaper coal be bought in from other places, where it is providing jobs for people in less economically developed countries (LEDCs) such as Colombia?
- Natural gas causes less air pollution than coal when burnt in power stations. Is it better to import natural gas from Russia to burn in power stations, or should local coal be used as it provides employment and wealth?

Focus on...
Tantalum

A little-known metal called tantalum has become important because of its use in the electronic components of computers, mobile phones and other devices. It is an exceptionally hard metal with a high electrical conductivity, hence its use in electronics. It has a high melting point of 3,017°C, so it can be used in the manufacture of alloys found in jet engines and nuclear power stations. At times, the price of tantalum has been as high as that of gold. Tantalum ores are found in many countries, including Australia, Canada and Brazil, but half the world's supply lies in the Democratic Republic of the Congo, where it occurs as an ore called columbium-tantalum or coltan.

▲ Tantalum is combined with nickel, cobalt and iron to make a super-alloy that can withstand the high temperatures of 3,000°C or more reached inside the combustion chamber of a jet engine.

Supply and Demand

Historically, the largest users of energy and raw materials are more economically developed countries (MEDCs) such as Germany, Japan, the United Kingdom and the United States. They need a constant supply of resources to fuel their economies, to generate growth and accumulate wealth. Several of these countries have exhausted many of their own natural resources, so they buy resources from other countries. However, there are some exceptions. Japan did not have a wealth of natural resources, for example, so instead it developed its wealth by investing in education and jobs, creating a large and educated workforce.

More recently, countries such as China, India and South Korea have also increased their consumption of the world's resources. This is heightening the demand for resources such as steel and copper, and pushing prices higher.

Natural resources are important to a country, especially LEDCs. However, to see any benefit the country has to extract those resources itself and not allow a third party to do it. Some politically unstable countries, such as Nigeria and Angola, have allowed their resources to be exploited by foreign companies or by elements of their own society so that wealth from the resources has not benefited the population as a whole. In contrast, many of the oil-producing countries of the Middle East have retained control over this important resource, and the whole country has seen an improvement in standards of living as a result.

▲ Oil was first discovered in the Gulf of Mexico in 1947. Since then more than 40,000 wells have been drilled. Recently a number of massive oil fields have been discovered that have boosted the United States oil reserves by more than 50 per cent.

Multinationals

Today, the supply of many natural resources lies in the hands of large corporations that operate in many different countries – the multinationals. Some of these own billions

▲ This oil refinery at Cochabamba in Bolivia was built by a Brazilian oil company, Petrobras, a company partly owned by the Brazilian government. Petrobras operates throughout the world.

Focus on...
Oil multinationals

In 2006, four of the top five largest corporations in the world, based on annual sales, were the oil companies ExxonMobil, Royal Dutch Shell, BP and Chevron. These corporations have long been involved with oil production. In recent years they have invested heavily in new oil fields in the Arctic, the Gulf of Mexico and the North Sea. Today they own or have leases in many oil fields around the world and they are actively carrying out research into new ways of drilling for oil, as well as investing in other energy sources such as renewables.

of dollars of assets and their annual earnings can even exceed those of individual countries. For example, in 2006 ExxonMobil reported the largest annual profit of any American company in history, a massive US$39.5 billion. In comparison, the country of Bolivia earned just US$10 billion and Costa Rica US$21 billion.

The size and wealth of the large multinationals mean that they have considerable power and they can influence political decisions, both in their home country and in the other countries in which they operate. They do this by donating to political parties and employing lobbyists – people who try to influence political decisions in favour of their employer or the group that they represent.

There are advantages and disadvantages to multinationals. Most multinational companies are owned by shareholders. This means that much of the profit made goes back to their shareholders. The countries in which the multinationals operate may see little of the profit. These companies also have a lot of buying power, so they can force prices down and put small, local companies out of business. However, the multinationals also create more employment opportunities, and

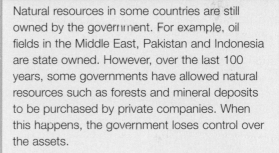

Have your say

Natural resources in some countries are still owned by the government. For example, oil fields in the Middle East, Pakistan and Indonesia are state owned. However, over the last 100 years, some governments have allowed natural resources such as forests and mineral deposits to be purchased by private companies. When this happens, the government loses control over the assets.

- Should all natural resources be owned by the state?
- Should private companies be forced to return their assets to the government?
- What effects might privatisation have on local economies?

the workforce may receive training and experience that benefits other parts of the local economy. The companies may have grant schemes to provide local entrepreneurs with money to set up their own businesses and to give them access to new technology and better work practices. Multinationals may finance new schools and hospitals.

Bad practice

In MEDCs, wages and standards of living are high. People may be protected by regulations concerning health and safety in the workplace, and these standards can be expensive to implement. The costs of extracting raw materials such as coal and iron, for example, are therefore high. Today, many companies source their natural resources from overseas, where the costs are much lower.

Chinese coal

One of the reasons resources are cheaper in LEDCs is the lower wages paid to workers. This comes at a price, though. China is the world's largest producer of coal but it also has one of the worst safety records. China's rapidly growing economy is putting pressure on mines to produce more coal. Here, miners earn a fraction of the salary of an American miner, less than US$1,000 a year compared

▲ The cost of labour is cheap in China. This coal mine does not use trains or trucks to move the coal. Instead people carry the coal from the mine to barges on a nearby river.

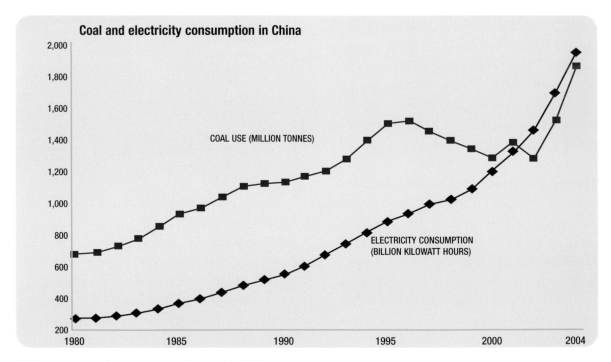

Coal and electricity consumption in China

COAL USE (MILLION TONNES)

ELECTRICITY CONSUMPTION (BILLION KILOWATT HOURS)

▲ This graph shows the increases in coal use and electricity demand in China. China is one of the largest coal-producing countries in the world.

with about US$40,000. The output of a Chinese miner is much lower, too – just over 300 tonnes per year compared with 15,000 tonnes in the United States. Machinery is used in American mines to boost output, but in China it is cheaper to employ more people. More money is saved by not implementing safety measures. As a result there are thousands of accidents in the mines. In 2005 about 6,000 miners died. There is also a lack of environmental controls, leading to air and water pollution as well as habitat loss.

Nigerian oil

Nigeria is one of the richest African countries in terms of natural resources, but the people have one of the poorest standards of living. Just less than half the country's earnings comes from oil in the Niger Delta. The oil operations have had considerable impact on the local people and wildlife of the delta, which is a huge wetland area considered to be of international importance.

For much of the last 30 years Nigeria was under the control of the military, which overruled everybody's wishes in its pursuit of wealth from oil. They brought in multinational companies and ignored the rights of the local people. Although the oil brings in money, local people see little benefit. Many still live in poverty and without access to clean water. Although the oil companies are not directly responsible for the problems, they have allowed the delta to be damaged. Toxic waste has been dumped in the delta and oil spills are frequent. There is strong opposition to the oil companies, and many local people support the militant groups who blow up pipelines and kidnap oil workers in a bid to force the oil companies to leave.

Eyewitness

'We believe we can help development most by: producing the oil and gas needed for economic development, supporting the government's development programme in the region, implementing our Sustainable Community Development strategy, combating corruption and improving our environmental performance.'
Basil Omiyi, Managing Director, Shell in Nigeria

'It is like paradise and hell. They have everything. We have nothing. If we protest, they send soldiers. They sign agreements with us and then ignore us. We have graduates going hungry, without jobs and they bring people from Lagos to work here.'
Eghare Ojhogar, chief of the Ugborodo community, Niger Delta

▲ Numerous small oil spills in the Niger Delta have polluted the water, causing a decline in fishing and the quality of drinking water. People of the Ijaw tribe say they have not been given any compensation by the oil companies.

▲ In 2006 President Evo Morales of Bolivia announced that the government was taking control of the country's oil resources. Bolivian soldiers were sent to the oil refineries and other distribution centres to make sure that the oil supply was not interrupted.

Getting it right

Fortunately there are also examples of good practice, which have enabled local communities to benefit from their natural resources. In the past, many of the resources obtained from LEDCs were shipped elsewhere for refining or for processing into goods, which would then be sold globally. Often the goods were sold back to the country from which the raw materials had been obtained, but at vastly increased prices. There are real benefits to be gained if the resources are processed locally, for example if aluminium smelters are located close to bauxite mines, or crude oil is refined close to the oil fields. Not only does this bring more jobs to the area, it also enables the community to add value to the natural resource. They can then trade the more valuable product with other parts of the world. For example, the only aluminium smelter in Southeast Asia is located in Indonesia. The smelter is jointly owned by a number of Japanese companies and the Indonesian government. Bauxite from Papua and Australia is processed using electricity generated from a hydroelectric power station, and the aluminium is sold in Japan and other Southeast Asian countries.

Taking back control

Governments of a number of LEDCs once sold off their country's assets to foreign companies. Now some of these governments are trying to take back control of these assets. For example, the governments of Bolivia and Venezuela are planning to nationalise their country's oil fields – that is, take them back into public ownership. This means that they will be able to manage their resources and earn money from them. Venezuela plans that the national oil company owned by the government will either own or have a majority share of the country's major oil fields. In Bolivia, many people feel that the foreign companies have plundered their reserves of natural gas, oil, tin and silver. The government is planning to keep more than 80 per cent of their oil revenues, but this is likely to put off any oil company from investing in Bolivia. Not surprisingly, the foreign oil companies are fighting these proposals. Ideally, there should be a balance so that both the country and the investor benefit.

The gap between rich and poor

Unfortunately there are some countries that have very few natural resources. There are also countries that have natural resources which have not been used due to political instability. For example, Somalia and Sudan have oil and small deposits of precious metals. However, civil wars have displaced millions of people in these areas and this, combined with drought, has left both populations in extreme poverty. These countries have seen few benefits from globalisation and now they are even poorer than they were a few years ago. The gap between the richest and the poorest countries has grown.

Have your say

In the past, many indigenous peoples were forced off their tribal lands so the natural resources could be exploited by others.

• Should the indigenous people be able to claim back land that has been part of their heritage?
• Does it matter how long ago it was taken?
• If the land is given back, should the private companies that now 'own' the natural resources of the land be compensated?

Focus on...
Claiming it back

In the past, it was not unusual for indigenous people to be moved from their traditional tribal lands following the discovery of valuable resources, such as oil and gold, or to make way for logging. Most were not compensated, nor did they receive a share of the profits. Now, several indigenous groups are campaigning for the right to claim back their tribal lands and the natural resources. The Bushmen of Botswana live in the Kalahari Game Reserve, a huge area protected especially for the Bushmen. In 1980 diamonds were found in the central area and the government forced the Bushmen to leave. After many years of campaigning, the Bushmen finally won the right to return to their tribal lands in 2006.

▲ Roy Sesana, leader of the Bushmen, celebrates their victory outside the High Court in Botswana in 2006. The court ruled that the government had wrongfully removed more than 2,000 bushmen from their ancestral lands.

Trees – a Sustainable Resource?

Wood is a valuable resource that has been used for thousands of years. It can be used in construction, to make paper and as a fuel. Five thousand years ago more than half the Earth's surface was covered by forest. Now it is just 20 per cent – about five billion hectares. Deforestation is still increasing and if it continues, many countries will soon have no forest left. Most valuable are primary forests – these are forests that have never been cleared and replanted. They are often called 'old-growth' forests and they have the highest biodiversity. The United Nations estimates that about 13 million hectares of the world's forests are lost each year, of which six million hectares are primary forest. Nigeria has the world's highest deforestation rate of just over 11 per cent, while Brazil loses the largest area of forest each year compared with other countries – more than three million hectares. Russia has the third largest annual loss of primary forest, and the United States has the seventh largest.

Disappearing forests

Tropical rainforests, with their high-quality timber trees such as mahogany and teak, are found close to the Equator. These dense forests have the highest biodiversity of any habitat. Further north, there is a huge belt of conifer trees across northern North America, Europe and Asia. The softwood from these fast-growing trees is used to make pulp for

▼ Wood is one of the most fundamental resources and has thousands of uses for humans. However, increases in demand for wood products have seen vast areas of forest being cleared.

paper and cardboard and for cheap timber. Both types of forest are being cleared at increasing rates. However, it is not all bad news. There was a drop of 40 per cent in the rate of deforestation in the Amazon between 2004 and 2006, taking it back to the level of the late 1990s.

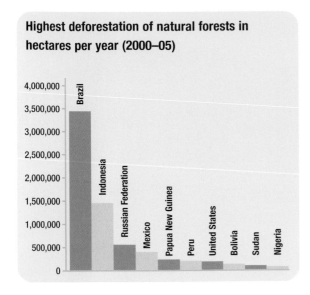

Highest deforestation of natural forests in hectares per year (2000–05)

Bars (left to right): Brazil (~3,450,000), Indonesia (~1,450,000), Russian Federation (~550,000), Mexico (~400,000), Papua New Guinea (~250,000), Peru, United States, Bolivia, Sudan, Nigeria

▲ This logging camp is in Russia. Some of the timber will be used for pulp and paper and the rest may be exported to countries such as China and India.

Looking for cheap timber

In North America and Europe, many of the older forests have been cleared and much of the remaining forest is protected. There are also strict laws concerning the use of forestry resources. This has forced many companies to look elsewhere for cheap supplies of timber. One such region is north-east Russia, a poor area that desperately needs jobs. Widespread clearance is now taking place with little control and it is destroying one of the few remaining habitats of the Siberian tiger. All over Russia, forests are under threat. The northern taiga was the world's largest expanse of forest, stretching across northern Russia. Now less than one quarter of this wilderness remains untouched by human activities. Tropical rainforests are also being cleared, especially in areas that were once considered too remote, such as Papua New Guinea and central Borneo.

Widespread effects

Deforestation can have surprisingly widespread consequences. The water runs off the bare land into streams and rivers, rather than being evaporated back into the atmosphere. This can cause flooding in some areas but reduced rainfall in others. Extensive deforestation in the Himalayas is causing more water to drain into rivers such as the Brahmaputra, which runs through India into Bangladesh. This is causing flooding in Bangladesh.

Focus on...
Illegal logging

Much deforestation is caused by illegal logging. The World Bank estimates that illegal logging costs governments and forest industries as much as US$15 billion every year. Each year, about 40 per cent of forest clearance is carried out illegally. Many countries pass laws to protect their forests and issue logging permits, but they do not police the forests. Poorly paid local officials can be easily bribed into allowing logging to take place. The forests are often in remote places so it is easy carry out illegal logging operations without being caught. Not only is valuable forest habitat lost through this practice, but the money from the timber does not go back into the local economy. Nobody but the illegal loggers gain.

▲ These pine seedlings in a tree nursery in the United States will be harvested in about 20–30 years' time, providing a sustainable supply of timber.

Sustainable forests

Globally, the demand for wood is outstripping the supply. With so much of the world's forest already cleared, it is important that the remaining forests are managed for the future.

Forestry makes up four per cent of international trade and in many countries it is a major source of income and employment. For example, about 100,000 people are employed by forestry companies in Sarawak, Malaysia. Many forests are state owned and governments issue logging permits to companies. However, these logging permits tend to be short term and there is no incentive for the company to invest in and manage the forests for the future. Less than one per cent of the world's rainforests are managed sustainably, so there is still much work to be done.

Replanting forests

Wood is a renewable resource and trees can be grown like crops. Fast-growing trees, such as pine and spruce, can be planted and allowed to grow for up to 40 years, then harvested and new ones planted in their place. In the past the trees would have been clear felled – that is, all the trees would be felled and the area replanted. Now the forests are managed so that some trees are left to provide cover for wildlife. Some countries have reforestation campaigns, for example between 2000 and 2005 more than 20 million hectares of trees were planted in China.

Forest stewardship

When a consumer buys a piece of timber, there is no way of knowing if the tree was logged illegally. To help consumers make informed choices, there are now schemes that identify wood that comes from forests that are managed sustainably. One such scheme is the FSC (Forest Stewardship Council). Wood meeting the standards of the FSC is labelled with the FSC logo so people buying it can be confident that it has been legally felled.

Local benefits

One way to ensure the survival of a forest is to give local people a reason to protect it. For example, they could be taught that they can earn money every year from the forest by harvesting wild fruits or nuts. Felling a forest only gives short-term gain. Once the forest is gone, there will be no more income. With careful management, such as only felling a few trees or planting new ones, there can be income every year. It may also be possible to market other products such as exotic fruits, or earn income from ecotourism.

Environmental benefits

Forests have high biodiversity, particularly the primary forests. However, protecting the forests doesn't just help wildlife. Forests have a key role to play in the water cycle and the global climate. The roots of trees hold the soil in place and take up water. They act as sponges by holding the water and releasing it slowly through the year. Once the protective tree cover is lost, the soil is easily eroded by wind and water. Water runs off the ground and into streams and rivers, where it may cause flooding. There is no evaporation of water from the trees back into the atmosphere and this can result in reduced rainfall.

Focus on...
Health drinks

The açai palm is found in Brazil. Local people have long known that its berries were good for health. Now it is being made into a health drink that is sold in Europe and North America. Its increased demand has created new jobs. There are more collectors in the forest, and new factories where the berries are crushed and made into a juice. In the past these palms were felled for their hearts, which were a delicacy. Now it is far more profitable to protect the palms and collect the berries, so the popularity of the açai drink is protecting the forests.

▲ The juice of açai berries is extracted by first soaking them in water to soften the skin, and then crushing them to extract the purple juice. The juice is an important part of the diet of Amazonian people, as it is rich in minerals and vitamins.

Controlling Trade

With 193 countries in the world all trading with each other, it is essential to have some rules and a forum (talking place) in which discussion can take place. Today, one of the key players in regulating world trade is the World Trade Organisation (WTO). This was set up in 1995 and it now has 150 members, all governments of countries. The main role of the WTO is to provide a forum, where its members can prepare international agreements on trade and settle trade disputes. Its aim is to make trade as easy as possible, with no unfair barriers. For this reason the WTO is closely linked to globalisation.

World trade
The WTO has helped to bring down trade barriers between countries, for example, by removing the import taxes on goods from certain countries and by lifting restrictions on the volume of goods that can be imported from another country. The WTO makes sure that one country does not discriminate by favouring particular nations. Members have agreed to abide by a set of rules. If a member breaks the rules, then the other members can act against them, for example by boycotting their goods, or by placing import taxes on their exports.

One country that has benefited greatly from membership of the WTO is China. China became a member in 2000 and since then has found it easier to export goods. Until that time, Chinese exporters faced trade barriers, as countries feared competition from China. Membership has enabled China take advantage of its low wages and large workforce to boost exports, and as a result it has become the world's third largest trading country. As exports have risen, so have imports. China has a huge demand for raw materials and imports of oil, copper and aluminium have risen steeply. Currently China uses about 20 per cent of the world's copper supply.

Trading commodities
A commodity is a raw material or agricultural product that is traded. Resources such as copper, oil and timber are examples of commodities. Today, most of the world's natural resources are traded in virtual commodity marketplaces. Worldwide, there are about 75 markets, for example the London Metal Exchange, which trades in metals, and the New York Mercantile Exchange, which trades in energy and metals. It is here that the price of a commodity is agreed. Most sales are made on a 'future' basis. For example, a gas company may decide to buy a certain volume of gas at an agreed price many months before the gas is actually needed. The buyer hopes that it will be cheaper to fix the price in the spring when prices are lower, than wait until winter when prices go up. However, there is a risk that prices may fall. This type of trading

▲ Each year, the WTO holds high-level meetings for government ministers and these meetings frequently attract protesters. They hold rallies as close as possible to the venue of the meeting, in this case outside the US Embassy in Manila, Philippines in 2001.

involves a lot of risk, and businesses fail as a result of poor decisions. Equally, there are opportunities to make a lot of money. Consumers often complain that the price of oil or gas is too high. They see the prices of these commodities falling, but the price they are paying remains high. Usually this is because the prices were set many months earlier.

▲ Every day, traders at the New York Mercantile Exchange buy and sell billions of dollars' worth of metals and energy products.

Eyewitness

There is considerable debate about the benefits of WTO membership to African countries that have rich natural resources, but where many still live in poverty.

'Fairness in international trade will not only help a lot of countries in Africa economically, but it will also alleviate hunger and poverty on the continent. African countries will depend less on aid, if there is a fair international trade. Africa can compete in the global market, if the environment is conducive to do so.'
Omorodion Osula, Boston, United States

'As a Nigerian and an African, I don't expect much from the WTO. What I know for sure is that they will bring up policies that will make Africans poorer. Ghana sends cocoa to the developed world, then it comes back as chocolate, more expensive than the cocoa itself. This only makes the rich countries richer.'
Victor Owo, Eket, Nigeria

A valuable resource

Of all the natural resources traded in the world, oil makes up the largest amount in value. In recent years the price of oil has increased, but this has not stopped the rise in demand from cars and industry. Experts believe that demand in oil will increase by almost 50 per cent between 2003 and 2030, with half the rise in demand coming from Asian countries such as China and India.

Cost of oil

The price of oil is affected by many different factors. In times of tension, for example wars in the Middle East, the price rises. However, as the oil price rises, people start to cut back on their use of oil, by driving less or using other fuels. As demand falls, the price drops back, too. Some oil reserves are expensive to drill, so when prices increase these reserves

become worthwhile and more oil comes into the market and the price falls. There are constant fluctuations in price and demand.

Other sources of oil

Oil can be extracted from oil shale, a type of rock rich in a substance called kerogen and tar sands which contain bitumen. Oil shales represent a large reserve of oil, of which more than 60 per cent is found in the United States. The kerogen is extracted and heated to form oil and gas. However, this is a costly process and oil from oil shale is only economic if the price of oil is above US$40 a barrel. The rise in prices since 2005 has led to greater interest in this source of oil.

OPEC

One of the most important trade associations linked to oil is OPEC – the Organisation of

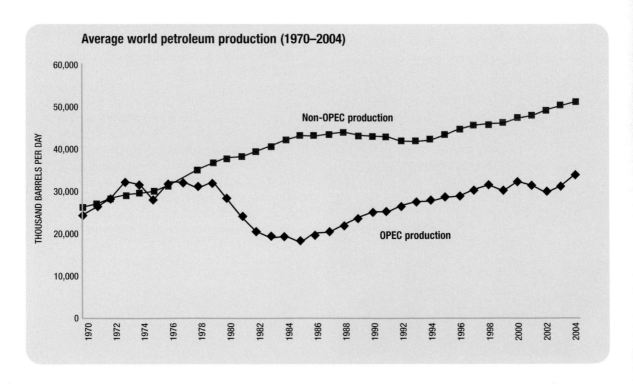

▲ This chart shows the average production of petrol between 1970 and 2004, split between OPEC and non-OPEC production.

Petroleum Exporting Countries. OPEC was formed in 1960 and currently there are 12 members: Algeria, Angola, Iraq, Indonesia, Iran, Kuwait, Libya, Nigeria, Qatar, Saudi Arabia, the United Arab Emirates and Venezuela. They produce about 40 per cent of the world's oil and they have about 70 per cent of the world's proven oil reserves. The role of OPEC is to coordinate the oil policies of the member countries. Although OPEC does not set a price for the oil, it influences the price by regulating its supply. It aims to ensure a steady supply of oil while obtaining a fair price for the producers.

▼ In 2006 wind energy powered three million homes in the United States and this number is increasing each year. It is hoped that by 2030 wind energy will generate 20 per cent of the country's electricity.

Focus on...
The 1973 oil crisis

In 1973, the world economy was thrown into crisis when the price of oil quadrupled within a few months. The crisis was triggered by the Yom Kippur War, in which Israel fought against Egypt and Syria. The Arab members of OPEC agreed not to supply oil to any country that supported Israel, particularly the United States. This caused an immediate shortage of oil and a staggering price rise. It caused the world economy to go into recession. However, the crisis forced governments to look to other sources of energy. In the United States, grants were made available for renewable energy projects, and numerous wind farms and solar power stations were built. After the crisis the oil price dropped back, but not to its original level.

Resource Wars

Natural resources have long been important in conflicts. Even in recent years, resources and trade routes have been the trigger for war. For example, the Gulf War (1990–91) started after Iraqi troops marched into Kuwait to capture the oil fields and gain a secure access to the Persian Gulf. Other conflicts occur over water or rights to valuable minerals.

▲ During the Gulf War the retreating Iraqi army tried to destroy the oil fields by setting alight wells and blowing up pipelines. Thick smoke and soot drifted over the region, while the groundwater was contaminated by oil. It took specialist teams many months to put out the fires.

Declining resources

As some resources start to decline, the remaining reserves will become increasingly important. There are limited supplies of oil and gas – once peak production is reached, the volume being traded will decline. Already governments and multinational corporations are setting up agreements to secure their supplies of oil and gas into the future.

Although the Middle East has the largest oil reserves, Russia also has substantial oil and gas reserves and is becoming increasingly important in the marketplace. Currently there are several Russian oil and gas pipelines supplying Europe and China. This places Russia in a powerful position to control the prices and even influence the economies of other countries. Some of the former Soviet states, such as the Ukraine, had enjoyed relatively cheap supplies of oil and gas, but in recent years Russia has raised the prices to market levels and caused economic problems.

Another problem is terrorism. Gas and oil fields, pipelines and the associated infra-structure are all terrorist targets. A well-placed bomb near a major pipeline could cause many months of interruption and environmental damage. For this reason the countries through which the pipelines pass have to make sure it is protected.

War-torn regions

Some rare mineral resources are only found in a few locations, so any instability in that region can interrupt the supply. One such example is the Democratic Republic of the Congo. This central African country is rich in natural resources, including timber, diamonds, copper, cobalt and coltan. In 1997 the government fell and there was a civil war. The mineral wealth attracted the attention of many neighbouring countries, who formed alliances

with local warlords and sent in troops. The civil war was financed by the illegal sales of minerals, especially diamonds and coltan, and during the conflict more than three million people died. In 2003, a peace deal was agreed, a new government was put in place and legal trade started again. However, there is still some fighting in the eastern end of the country.

Focus on...
Blood diamonds

Diamonds are valuable exports for a number of African countries. However, the illegal trade in diamonds has funded civil wars in countries such as Angola and Sierra Leone. International action has taken place to make sure that trade in the so-called 'blood diamonds' stops. Although the United Nations has placed sanctions on a number of these countries, it took action by the diamond industry itself to stop the trade. In 2001 a new organisation called the World Diamond Council was set up. Its role was to make sure that all diamonds sold around the world have a certificate proving that they came from legitimate diamond mines.

▼ Many diamonds are found in a rock called kimberlite. The rock is removed from the ground and crushed to release the diamonds. Those of sufficient quality to become gems are cut and polished, a process that can reduce the size of the diamond by half.

Water rights

A person's access to water is described as a fundamental human right. However, by 2025, the demand for water may rise by 40 per cent and nearly two-thirds of the world's population will live in regions where the demand for water outstrips the supply. This may be a result of climate change, or simply a lack of infrastructure, for example inadequate water-distribution systems for piping water to the people. As demand for water increases, disputes between countries over their right to water may become more common.

Sharing resources

River water has many uses – as a source of drinking water, for irrigating crops, for industrial processes, power generation and much else. However, rivers often run through several countries. There is the risk that upstream countries will take too much of the water, leaving countries downstream with insufficient supplies. For example the Mekong is the longest river in Asia. It is just under 5,000 km long, rising in China and then crossing Burma, Thailand, Laos, Cambodia and Vietnam. Barely 20 years ago, the Mekong was described as being virtually untouched. Now the building of dams, together with increasing water demands from these fast-growing countries, is having considerable influence on the river. The level of water is lower and there are fewer fish. Other major rivers in the world are experiencing similar pressures.

Water treaties

One way to resolve the dispute is by drawing up a water treaty, so that all parties know

▼ Glen Canyon Dam on the Colorado River was completed in 1963. The dam created a huge reservoir called Lake Powell. Here, the authorities are releasing water from the lake to stimulate a flood. The extra water helps to move silt down the river, mimicking a natural process.

exactly how much water can be drawn from the river. One of the first treaties was the Colorado River Compact in 1922. The Compact details how much water can be extracted from the Colorado River as it flows through seven American states before entering Mexico. Over the years the terms have been altered to accommodate a change in demand, but several disputes have had to be settled in court. A further agreement was drawn up between the United States and Mexico, giving Mexico the right to withdraw water.

Although the treaty considered people's requirements, the needs of wildlife were overlooked. So much water has been extracted that wildlife of the Colorado Delta in Mexico has suffered greatly. Once it was a

wetland teeming with wildlife, but the building of almost 60 dams, together with numerous water-diversion projects, means that the delta receives just a trickle of water.

Focus on...
Polluted rivers

Water pollution is another cross-border issue. If one country releases toxic chemicals into a river, it is very difficult for neighbouring countries downstream to stop the pollution. This happened recently in China. In November 2005 there was an explosion at a chemical plant in Jilin City, which lies on the Songhua River. This river drains into the Amur, a major Russian river. The accident created an 80-km long toxic slick that moved downstream, affecting a number of Chinese cities including Harbin, a city of three million people. The water was so toxic that Harbin city officials cut off the water supply for a week and brought in water by truck.

▼ This worker is collecting the litter that is floating down the Li River in China.

Too little water

The amount of water flowing down a river depends on many factors. After heavy rain there can be excessively high water levels and flooding, while after a drought the water levels fall. Also, the water level in a river can fall following the construction of a dam, because so much water is trapped in the reservoir behind the dam. Countries lying downstream usually find that the water level is out of their control.

Most water treaties are drawn up on the assumption that there will be a surplus of water. However, problems start when there is a drought. Then the water flow is greatly reduced and the river may even dry up completely. All the countries along the length of the river want water, so who has to go without? The Rivers Tigris and Euphrates in the Middle East are good examples. About two-thirds of the river water comes from Turkey and the rest from Syria. Both rivers run through Iraq, providing the country with

Have your say

When the Three Gorges Dam on the Yangtze River in China is finished in 2009, it will be the world's largest hydroelectric dam and will create a reservoir just under 600 km long. It will supply one-ninth of China's electricity.

• Are the benefits of clean electricity more important that the rights of the millions of people who will be moved from their homes?
• The dam will alter the river and affect wildlife. Is it better to dam rivers to generate electricity than build new nuclear power stations?

all its water. Although there is a treaty in place, all three countries want more water, especially Turkey. Turkey has plans to increase the number of dams in the region, to generate more than half the country's electricity. In 1990, the filling of the reservoir behind the new Ataturk Dam on the Euphrates left Syria and Iraq short of water,

▼ The Hoover Dam on the Colorado River is an example of how water is being used as a renewable resource to generate hydroelectricity.

▲ The Indus River (on the left of this picture) rises in Tibet and flows through the Himalayas into India before turning south into Pakistan. The level of water varies through the year. It is low in winter and then rises as the snow melts in spring. It swells again after the heavy monsoon rains in summer.

and Syria was forced to shut down several hydroelectric power stations. The problems continue as all three countries have increased their water use but the flow of water has not increased by the same amount.

Problems of dams

Hydroelectric power is a renewable source of energy, and many countries are looking at their water resources with the aim of generating clean hydroelectricity However, giant dams can have a considerable effect on the flow of water downstream. When the Hoover Dam was built on the Colorado River, Lake Mead was formed behind it. Care had to be taken when filling the lake, as the dam has the potential to store two-years' worth of river water behind it. Similar problems are being experienced in Southeast Asia, where the flow of water along the Mekong River has been greatly reduced by giant dams along the Chinese stretch of the river. China gains water for its growing population and electricity, but Thailand, Laos,

Focus on...
The Indus River

The Indus River rises in Tibet, and flows through Pakistan to the Arabian Sea, a distance of 2,900 km. Pakistan depends on the river for virtually all its water. However, some of the rivers flowing into the Indus rise in India. The Indus Water Treaty was agreed in 1960 following a water dispute between the two countries. Until recently both countries had abided by the terms of the treaty. However, in 1999 India started work on a hydroelectric dam on the River Chenab and Pakistan claimed that the dam would reduce water flow, leaving less for agriculture and their own hydroelectric schemes. An independent expert was appointed by the World Bank to judge the case and he found in favour of the Indians, so the dam can be completed.

Cambodia and Vietnam are experiencing lower river levels. This is affecting fishing and river transport, and is causing a loss of the silt that maintains the fertility of riverside fields.

35

Environmental Damage

Virtually all the stages in the extraction and processing of natural resources have the potential to cause environmental damage. Sometimes the pollution is restricted to the local region but more often it affects a wide area or even the whole planet. When this happens, action to reduce the damage has to be global too.

Mining and the local environment

Mining for resources such as bauxite, coal and uranium always causes environmental damage. Strip mining is particularly destructive as large areas of soil are removed to reveal the rock below. This form of environmental damage is not restricted to LEDCs; it is still taking place in parts of Europe and the United States. In the Appalachian Mountains in the United States, coal-mining companies use huge earth movers to clear soil in order to reach the coal. In some places whole mountain tops have been cleared. The spoil is pushed into valleys and the land is levelled. The devastation is widespread. However, the mining companies claim that they generate jobs, that it takes place in remote locations and that flattening the land makes it more useful.

▼ This strip mine in the Appalachian Mountains in the United States is removing layers of coal from the top of this mountain. Often the waste is bulldozed into valleys, blocking rivers.

Global support network

Many companies involved in oil exploration or mineral extraction are finding it increasingly difficult to operate in MEDCs due to tighter environmental laws, higher operating costs and considerable public opposition. Consequently, some companies have moved their operations to other parts of the world where there are weaker environmental laws.

Not surprisingly, local people want to stop this. In the past they did not have much of a voice but this is changing. People are using the Internet to communicate and to campaign. For example, the people of Kashipur in India are battling with the giant Canadian company Alcan over plans to develop a huge bauxite mine. More than 20,000 people will lose their homes and the environment will be irreversibly damaged. The local people have received support from people all around the world, including Alcan workers in Canada.

Focus on...
Mercury

Small operations can be just as damaging as large ones. For example, just under half of the world's gold comes from small-scale mining operations in countries such as Brazil, Colombia, Indonesia and Tanzania. The miners use mercury, a highly toxic substance, to extract the gold. Unfortunately, the mercury gets washed into streams and rivers. Major rivers such as the Nile, Mekong, Amazon and Zambesi have all been affected by mercury. Mercury has even ended up in international waters. The mercury is taken up by fish, mussels and other aquatic animals that are eaten by people. Aid organisations are educating the miners in alternative methods that recycle the mercury.

▼ Small-scale gold mining such as this in Colombia creates considerable environmental damage, as the miners often use mercury to extract the gold. This is a risk to their health and to the water quality.

Global action

Pollution knows no boundaries. Sulphur dioxide released by a power station in one country may be carried hundreds of kilometres by the wind and cause acid rain in another country. Therefore, action to prevent many forms of pollution has to be international.

There have been a number of initiatives to tackle environmental problems. After it was proved that chlorofluorocarbons (CFCs) were damaging the ozone layer, 43 countries agreed to phase out these chemicals. In 1999, 27 European countries signed an agreement to cut a range of gases that contribute to air pollution.

Another milestone was the Earth Summit in 1992 – a hugely successful conference organised by the United Nations to discuss the global environment, climate change and sustainable development.

Acid rain

During the 1980s images of dying forests and dead fish hit the headlines. The cause was acid rain. The main culprit was coal-burning power stations, which released sulphur dioxide into the atmosphere. This reacted with water to create acid rain.

Since this time there has been regional action to combat the problem. This action has included Clean Air Acts to control sulphur-dioxide emissions, and requirements to put filters in the chimneys of coal-burning power stations to remove the sulphur dioxide. As a result, sulphur-dioxide emissions have fallen across North America and Europe. However, in newly industrialised countries such as India and China, acid rain is a growing problem.

Global warming

One international problem hitting the headlines is global warming. This is an issue that faces us all, but not everyone will be affected to the same extent. Although people and industries in MEDCs have caused much of the problem, these countries are more likely to be able to cope with the effects, as there is money and technology available to overcome the problems. It is people in LEDCs that will bear the brunt of the problem. For example, people in Bangladesh will suffer from rising sea levels that will flood low-lying areas, and the likelihood of more severe cyclones (tropical storms), while people in Tanzania may experience severe droughts that will cause crops to fail and cause starvation. These people do not have the financial resources and access to technology to overcome the changes. It is here that money has to be invested to enable people to adapt.

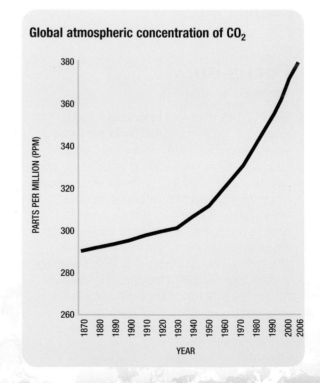

Global atmospheric concentration of CO_2

PARTS PER MILLION (PPM)

YEAR

Focus on...
The Kyoto Protocol

The Kyoto Protocol is an international agreement to reduce emissions of greenhouse gases such as carbon dioxide. The 175 countries that have signed this Protocol produce about 55 per cent of the world's greenhouse-gas emissions. During the period 2008–12, the industrialised countries have pledged to cut their emissions of greenhouse gases to 5.2 per cent below the 1990 levels. The other group of countries includes Brazil, China and India, and less developed countries. They are not required to make any reductions yet. Unfortunately Australia and the United States have not agreed to the Protocol.

Eyewitness

'Most of the observed increase in globally averaged temperatures in recent decades is very likely due to the observed increase in human-caused greenhouse-gas concentrations.'
IPCC (Intergovernmental Panel on Climate Change) Report, 2007

'There are many more important problems in the world to worry about, such as diseases, pandemics, nuclear war and terrorism. The least important of these is global warming produced by humans, because it will be insignificant compared to natural fluctuations of climate.'
Fred Singer, president of the Science and Environmental Policy Project research group, a group of scientists dedicated to providing objective, science-based information on a wide range of environmental issues

▼ In 2004 more than 33 million people in Bangladesh were affected by five weeks of flooding following the annual monsoon rains. Extreme weather events such as this could become more common.

Future issues

As demand for resources increases, especially in the fast-developing countries of India and China, there is likely to be even more environmental damage. Resources have to be managed sustainably so that they do not run out and to ensure the environment is protected.

Reducing, re-using and recycling

People living in MEDCs are incredibly wasteful. Each year, billions of tonnes of waste are thrown away, much of which is either buried or burnt. This represents a waste of valuable resources. A better way forward is for people to use fewer resources. If this is not possible, then waste needs to be either re-used or recycled. This way fewer resources need to be taken from the ground and less energy used to process them.

Have your say

Airline flights are among the fastest-growing sources of global-warming gases.

- Do you think governments should limit the number of flights you take each year?
- Should aviation fuel be taxed in the same way as petrol?

No more fossil fuels

History has shown that if a resource becomes scarce, people are very good at getting around the problem by inventing new ways to do things. Some countries have decided that they want a move towards a fossil-fuel free society, relying on other energy sources and technical innovations to solve the problems that the lack of fossil fuels will cause. The changeover

▼ In MEDCs, the most common way of disposing of rubbish is in holes in the ground called landfills. However, so much waste has been generated that the landfills are filling up, so alternative means of disposal will soon be needed.

won't be quick – experts reckon is will take up to 50 years, but it can happen. One such society is Iceland. Two-thirds of the energy there already comes from clean sources such as geothermal and hydroelectric, and the government is now tackling the rest. It thinks the fuel of the future is hydrogen, so it plans to make hydrogen using clean energy sources. Then the hydrogen will be used to power cars and heat buildings.

Looking forward

So what does the future hold for issues of environmental protection? The answer may be surprising. MEDCs and various non-government organisations (NGOs) could continue to provide financial help for environmental protection in LEDCs, but the most sustainable approach is likely to be through trade. With the removal of trade barriers, the lifting of subsidies and quotas, and with increased investment in industry, many LEDCs will be able to increase their trade. As the wealth of a country increases, so too does the standard of living and more money is available to invest in the environment.

Focus on...
Prototype Carbon Fund

It is important that investment is made into new technology for reducing emissions and harnessing renewable energy. Leading the way is the Prototype Carbon Fund, which was established by the World Bank in 2000. The PCF invests money from 17 energy companies and six governments into projects mostly in LEDCs that reduce emissions.

▼ Geothermal energy is used to heat almost 90 per cent of homes in Iceland. Here waste warm water from the geothermal plant is put to recreational use in the Blue Lagoon.

The Great Debate

Globalisation has made it easier for natural resources to be traded around the world. The level of trade as increased too, especially in key resources such as oil, iron and copper. Natural resources are so critical to a country's economy that they can cause conflict. However, the trade has also resulted in more environmental damage.

Advantages include:

● A wider range of resources are now being traded.

● More countries are becoming involved in the trade of resources.

● The globalisation of trade in resources has created more employment in less developed parts of the world.

● This trade brings wealth to a country and raises standards of living, so fewer people live in poverty.

● More money is generated that can be spent dealing with environmental issues.

● Trade means that LEDCs are less dependent on aid and loans.

Disadvantages include:

● Globalisation has made it easier for large companies to grow even larger and to exert more power in the marketplace.

● The multinational companies make it difficult for small, local companies to compete in a global market.

● Fewer employment laws in some LEDCs have enabled some companies to manufacture goods at low cost by paying low wages to their workers.

● Weaker environmental laws in some LEDCs have led to widespread environmental damage.

● Resources are not always managed sustainably.

● The high value of some resources has led to conflict.

Facts and Figures

- Between 2000 and 2005 the annual net loss of forest area was just over seven million hectares, an area the size of Sierra Leone. This is based on 13 million hectares being cleared and six million hectares of new forest, either natural or planted.

- Forest plantations occupy less than five per cent of the world's forested area, but provide 20 per cent of the world's wood production.

- Coal is used to generate 40 per cent of the world's electricity, oil generates 10 per cent, natural gas 15 per cent, nuclear power 16 per cent, hydro and renewables 19 per cent.

- Coal deposits are found in approximately 50 countries. In 2004, the annual coal production was just over 4,000 million tonnes. Coal production has increased by almost 40 per cent since 1984.

- In 2006, it was estimated that there were oil reserves of about 1,300 billion barrels, of which about 70 per cent were in Canada and the Middle East, according to the *Oil and Gas Journal*.

- In 1998 the US Geological Survey estimated world reserves of copper at about 350 million tonnes. However, new deposits are being found each year. In 2006 the world's fifth largest copper and gold reserves were discovered in Pakistan.

- The most optimistic estimates predict that coal will last another 252 years, gas 72 years and oil 32 years if they continue to be used at the rates they are now.

- In a modern city, water use is between 300 and 600 litres per person. This compares to less than 40 litres per day per person in the driest regions of the world.

- Canada uses the most energy per capita of all the countries in the world. LEDCs only account for 30 per cent of global total energy consumption.

Further Information

Books

Climate Change Begins at Home: Life on the Two-Way Street of Global Warming
by Dave Reay (Palgrave Macmillan, 2006)

Environments (Sustainable World)
by Rob Bowden (HodderWayland, 2003)

Power: Ethical Debates in Resources and the Environment (Dilemmas in Modern Science)
by Kate Ravilious (Evans Brothers, 2008)

Science at the Edge: Alternative Energy Supplies
by Sally Morgan (Heinemann Library, 2002)

Sustainable Development
by Clive Gifford (Heinemann Library, 2004)

Sustainable Futures series
by various authors (Evans Brothers, 2006)

The Earth's Resources (Science on File)
by Richard Spilsbury and Louise Spilsbury (Evans Brothers, 2006)

The Energy Debate: Biomass Power
by Isobel Thomas (HodderWayland, 2007)

Websites

http://www.eia.doe.gov/
Energy Information Administration. US site with official statistics on energy use in the United States.

http://www.scienceonline.co.uk/energy/nonrenewable.html
Science Online. Webpages looking at non renewable energy sources.

http://www.geography.learnontheinternet.co.uk/topics/rainforest.html
Internet Geography. Useful resources on a range of topics including the future of the rainforests.

http://www.geographyinthenews.rgs.org/
Geography in the News. Website with lots of up-to-date information on geography, put together by the Royal Geographical Society.

http://rainforests.mongabay.com/
Monga bay – plenty of information on the rainforests.

http://www.chooseclimate.org/
The Choose Climate website allows you to calculate your own transport emissions.

http://www.foei.org/
Friends of the Earth. This website has lots of information on environmental issues, and how we can all help to preserve the Earth's natural resources.

Glossary

acid rain rain that is more acidic than usual, with a pH of less than 5.6, caused by sulphur dioxide and nitrous oxides dissolving in water in the atmosphere.

alloy a mixture of two or more metals. Alloys are often stronger than pure metals.

barrel a unit of volume used for oil, where one barrel equals 159 litres or 42 US gallons.

bauxite an ore of aluminium.

biodiversity the total number of different species of plants and animals living in a particular habitat.

civil war a war between groups of people living in the same country.

climate change the rise in global temperatures that is causing changes in the climate, including heavy rains and violent storms. Climate change takes place naturally, but human activities are increasing its rate. The burning of fuels that interfere with the natural balance of gases in the atmosphere is largely to blame.

commodity a raw material or agricultural product that is traded.

conservation the active management of the Earth's natural resources and the environment to ensure their quality is maintained and that they are wisely used.

crude oil liquid oil as it is found beneath the surface of the Earth. Crude oil contains many other substances so is taken to a refinery to separate the components.

deforestation the clearance of forests from an area.

economy the supply of money gained by a community or country from goods and services.

ecotourism tourism designed to educate visitors about places of historic or natural interest and which is conducted in such a way that it benefits these sites and local communities.

entrepreneur an individual who sets up his or her own business.

erosion the wearing away of a natural feature such as rock or soil by wind or water.

export any good or service that is sold outside the country in which it originates.

fossil fuel a carbon-rich fuel, formed over millions of years from the dead remains of living organisms.

globalisation the freedom of businesses to operate all over the world and to invest and employ workers wherever they choose.

habitat the place where a plant or animal lives.

import any good or service that originates outside the country in which it is purchased.

less economically developed country (LEDC) one of the poorer countries of the world. LEDCs include all of Africa, Asia (except Japan), Latin America and the Caribbean, and Melanesia, Micronesia and Polynesia

lignite a poor-quality brown coal with high levels of sulphur, and which releases a lot of sulphur dioxide when burnt.

more economically developed country (MEDC) one of the richer countries of the world. MEDCs include all of Europe, North America, Australia, New Zealand and Japan.

ore a mineral deposit from which metal can be extracted, for example aluminium can be extracted from the ore bauxite.

overburden layers of rock and soil that cover coal in the ground, which are removed during mining.

pollution the presence of high levels of harmful substances in the environment, often as a result of human activity.

quarry to dig useful rocks such as limestone or granite out of the ground.

quota a limit on the amount of a produce that can be imported into a country. Often used to protect domestic producers from cheaper or competing imported goods.

recession a period of economic decline or very slow growth.

recycle to process items such as bottles or cans so that the materials from which they are made can be used again.

refinery a factory where crude oil is separated into its component parts by heating.

renewable energy energy that is generated from sources that can be replaced or renewed; renewable resources include wind and sun.

reserve something kept back for future use; the amount of a resource that is available for use.

resource something of value that can be put to a particular use – oil, coal and copper are examples of natural resources.

sanctions restrictions placed on trading goods or on financial dealings, usually as a result of a country trading unfairly with others.

seam a layer or bed of coal in the ground.

seismology the science of studying the structure of the Earth.

smelter a factory where an ore is heated to extract the pure metal.

subsidy a financial benefit paid to a producer as an incentive to produce. Subsidies are normally paid by government bodies and are especially used in farming.

sustainable using raw materials in such a way that their supply will continue into the future, without causing environmental damage.

wetlands lands made up of marshes or swamps.

Index